Kamala Harris

First Female Vice President of the United States

by Grace Hansen

Abdo
Kids

**HISTORY MAKER
BIOGRAPHIES**

abdobooks.com

Published by Abdo Kids, a division of ABDO, P.O. Box 398166, Minneapolis, Minnesota 55439.
Copyright © 2022 by Abdo Consulting Group, Inc. International copyrights reserved in all countries.
No part of this book may be reproduced in any form without written permission from the publisher.
Abdo Kids Jumbo™ is a trademark and logo of Abdo Kids.

Printed in the United States of America, North Mankato, Minnesota.

052021

092021

 THIS BOOK CONTAINS RECYCLED MATERIALS

Photo Credits: Alamy, AP Images, iStock, Shutterstock PREMIER, White House

Production Contributors: Teddy Borth, Jennie Forsberg, Grace Hansen
Design Contributors: Candice Keimig, Pakou Moua

Library of Congress Control Number: 2021932510
Publisher's Cataloging-in-Publication Data

Names: Hansen, Grace, author.

Title: Kamala Harris: first female Vice President of the United States / by Grace Hansen

Other title: first female Vice President of the United States

Description: Minneapolis, Minnesota : Abdo Kids, 2022 | Series: History maker biographies | Includes
    online resources and index.

Identifiers: ISBN 9781098208929 (lib. bdg.) | ISBN 9781098209063 (ebook) | ISBN 9781098209131
    (Read-to-Me ebook)

Subjects: LCSH: Harris, Kamala, 1964---Juvenile literature. | Women legislators--United States--Biography-
    -Juvenile literature. | Vice-presidents--United States--Biography--Juvenile literature. | United States.--
    Congress.--Senate--Biography--Juvenile literature.

Classification: DDC 328.73092--dc23

Table of Contents

Early Life & Education

Kamala Devi Harris was born on October 20, 1964, in Oakland, California.

California

Kamala's family lived in Berkeley, California. Her father, Donald, is Jamaican. He was a professor. Shyamala, her mother, was from India. She was a scientist.

When Kamala was 12, her parents divorced. She and her younger sister Maya moved with their mother to Quebec, Canada. There, Kamala finished middle school and high school.

In 1982, Kamala left for Washington, DC to attend college at Howard University. She then returned to California for law school. She graduated in 1989.

Career

Harris's first job was as a deputy district attorney. In 1998, she went to work with the San Francisco District Attorney's Office. In 2004, her hard work led to her becoming **district attorney** of San Francisco.

In 2010, Harris was **elected**

attorney general of California.

She was the first female and

Black person to earn the job!

In 2015, Kamala decided to run for **Senate**. Harris earned many votes and easily won the election. She took office as a United States senator in 2017.

17

In 2019, Kamala announced she would run for president of the United States. She later dropped out of the race. It wasn't long before Joe Biden asked Harris to be his **running mate**.

The First but Not the Last

In November of 2020, Harris was **elected** the first female vice president of the United States. She took office in January of 2021. She said, "While I may be the first woman in this office, I will not be the last."

21

Timeline

Harris graduates from Howard University with a degree in political science and economics.

Harris is hired as deputy district attorney in Alameda County, CA.

Harris takes office as the first female and first Black **attorney general** of California.

January 20
Kamala Harris becomes the first female vice president of the United States.

1986　　**1990**　　　　　　　**2011**　　**2021**

1964　　　　**1989**　　　　**2004**　　　　　**2017**

October 20
Kamala Devi Harris is born in Oakland, California.

Harris graduates from University of California, Hastings College of Law.

Harris takes office as the **district attorney** of San Francisco.

January 3
Kamala joins the United States **Senate**.

Glossary

attorney general – the principal legal officer who represents a country or state in legal proceedings and gives legal advice to the government.

district attorney – a public official who acts as prosecutor for the state or the federal government in court in a particular district.

elected – chosen by means of voting.

running mate – an election candidate for the lesser of two closely related political offices, for instance, a person running for president chooses a running mate who will become vice president.

Senate – one of the two houses of the United States Congress whose responsibilities include all lawmaking within the country.

Index

Abdo Kids
ONLINE
FREE! ONLINE MULTIMEDIA RESOURCES

Visit **abdokids.com**
to access crafts, games,
videos, and more!

Use Abdo Kids code

HJK8929

or scan this QR code!